Tenor Clef for the Cello

by Cassia Harvey

CHP109

www.charveypublications.com - print books
www.learnstrings.com - PDF downloadable books
www.harveystringarrangements.com - chamber music

Tenor Clef Notes

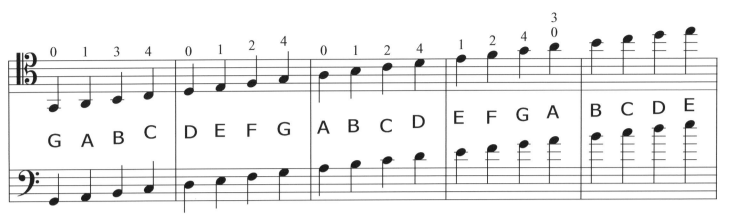

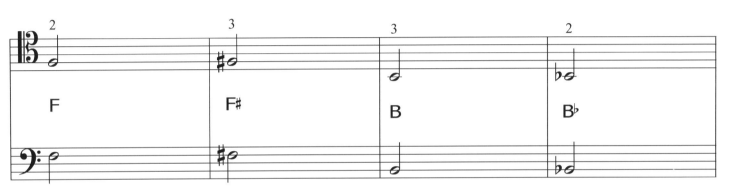

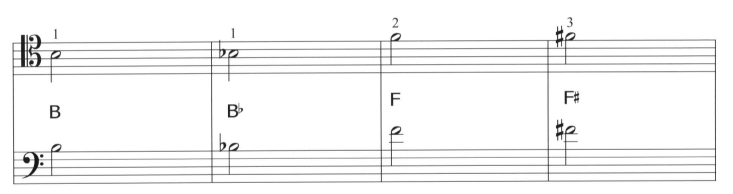

Open Strings

Fourth Position

Mid-String Harmonics

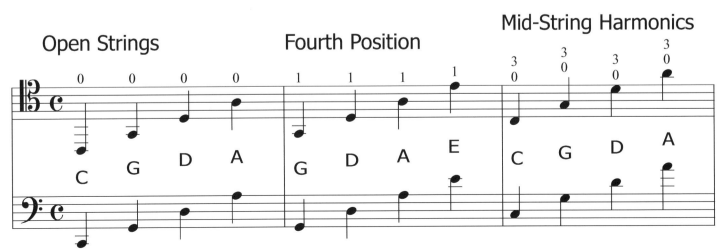

Tenor Clef for the Cello

I. The note "C"

Cassia Harvey

Finger Exercise

Suite

Purcell

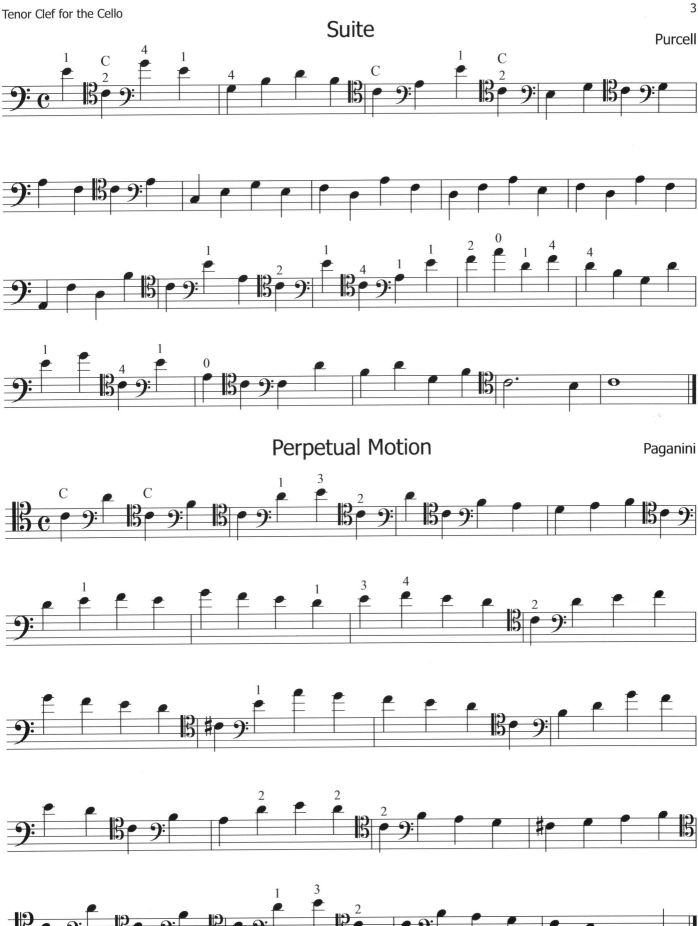

Perpetual Motion

Paganini

II. The note "B"

Finger Exercise

Spring: Allegro

Vivaldi

Spring: Pastorale

Vivaldi

III. The notes "D" and "A"

Finger Exercise

Minuet

Bach

Shifting Exercise

Barcarolle

Offenbach

IV. The notes "E" and "F#"

Across Strings

Scale

L'Arlesienne Suite

Bizet

Fine

D.C. al Fine

Don Giovanni

Mozart

V. The notes "F♮" and "G"

Across Strings

Tenor Clef for the Cello

Scales

G major

F major

Brandenburg No. 6

Bach

Alla Rustica

Vivaldi

VI. The notes "Low G" and "Low F#"

Finger Exercise

Minuet

Bach

Brandenburg No. 3

Bach

VII. The notes "High A" and "Low E"

Finger Exercise

Marcia

Bach

Pomp and Circumstance

Elgar

VIII. Using Tenor Clef

Put your own fingerings in.
Shift as little as possible.

Shifting

Perpetual Motion

Paganini

17

IX. The note "High B"

6th Position

7th Position

8th Position

Swan Lake

Tchaikovsky

Royal Fireworks Music

Handel

New World Symphony

Dvorak

20

Tenor Clef for the Cello

X. The note "High B♭"

Across Strings

©2018 C. Harvey Publications All Rights Reserved.

Rondeau

Purcell

XI. The note "High C"

Shifting to "High C"

Eine Kleine Nachtmusik: Allegro

Mozart

Eine Kleine Nachtmusik: Rondo

Mozart

XII. The note "High C#"

Shifting

Arkansas Traveler

Traditional

O Mio Babbino Caro

Puccini

XIII. The note "High D"

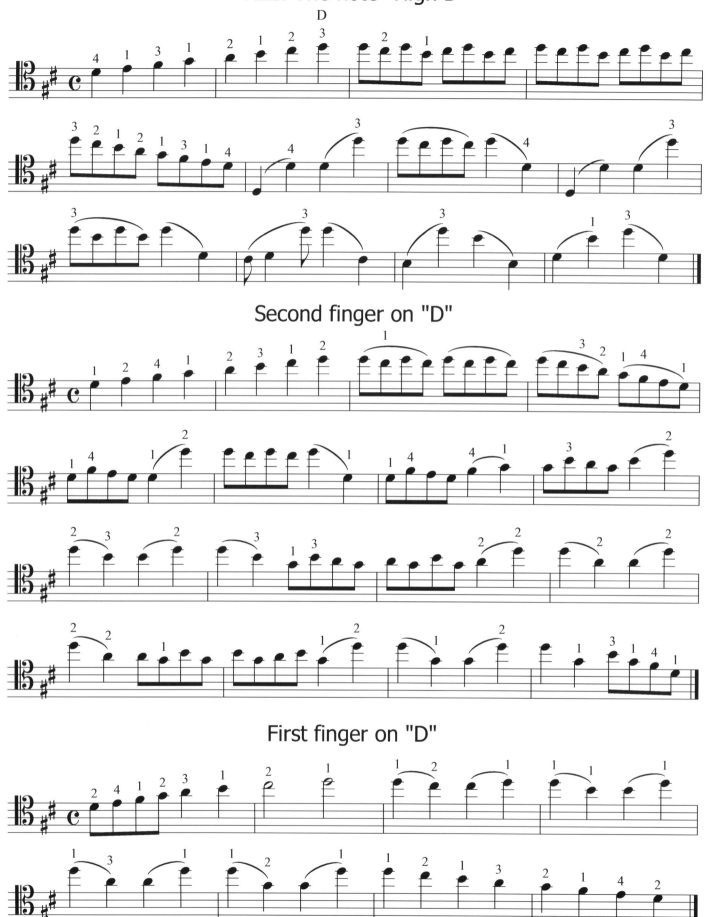

Second finger on "D"

First finger on "D"

Air

Handel

XIV. Fourths and Octaves

Bourree

Bach

Hornpipe

Handel

XV. Arpeggios

Bourree

Bach

XVI. Shifting Exercise

Dance of the Blessed Spirits

Gluck

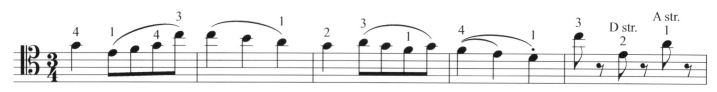

Etude #4

Wohlfahrt

Andante

Gavotte and Rondeau

Bach

Note: The Élégie is broken up into sections in this study book. The complete Élégie is at the back of the book.

Élégie
Part One: Measures 1-9

Élégie, Op. 24 by Gabriel Fauré
Exercises by Cassia Harvey

Key of C minor: B♭, E♭, A♭

Learning the Positions
Measures 2-5

Made in the USA
Las Vegas, NV
01 March 2024

86562774R00022